Pedigree

Published 2015. Pedigree Books Limited, Beech Hill House, Walnut Gardens, Exeter, Devon EX4 4DH. www.pedigreebooks.com – books@pedigreegroup.co.uk The Pedigree trademark, email and website addresses, are the sole and exclusive properties of Pedigree Group Limited, used under licence in this publication.

WELL, HELLO THERE AND WELCOME!

It's beginning to look a lot like 2016, and what better way to see in a brand new year than with the Griffins?

If you're having a year's-end identity crisis, they can relate. Particularly Peter. In Season 13, he's finding out that 'Peter' isn't actually his real name. You can read more about that in our brand new **episode guide** and create your own cool, new you with some **temporary tattoos**.

On the theme of identities, we're looking at (and liking) lookalikes.

There have certainly been a number of those on Family Guy over the years. Cast your eye over some of the strangest, in **Double Take**.

And talking of strange... Here are two words for you: Mayor West.

This year, we're celebrating the surreal with some of the most bizarre sentences he's ever uttered (and a **weird wordsearch**).

This year, Peter's been pretty busy with his social media activity. The photographic fruits of his (admittedly laid back) labour are on display in **Peter's Pictures**.

And, if you're keen to pursue a hobby or self-improvement path this year, get motivation of the Griffin kind with our **New Year's Resolutions** feature.

If you want to be Lois-level practical about it, plan your year Quahog-style with a **guide to the seasons.**

Or you could leave it all to the stars. Find out what's in store for you with your own - in-no-way-at-all-made-up (cough!) - **2016 horoscopes.**

Pssst! If you're reading this at Christmas, and a friend or relation's festive feasting is catching up with them fast, why not let them know you know, and give them possibly the best present ever: their own **greatest farter certificate!** Plus, in these pages, you'll also find out how to make your very own **Family Guy mug.** Exciting, huh? (No oven mitts for you!)

So what are you waiting for? Turn the page, and let's get started!

····························

BRIAN: Who the hell buys a novelty fire extinguisher?

PETER: I'll tell you who. Someone who cares enough about physical comedy to put his whole family at risk.

'A VERY SPECIAL FAMILY GUY FREAKIN' CHRISTMAS'

····························

CHRIS: Oven mitts! Wow! Thanks, Mom!

LOIS: Now you don't have to ask me if everything is hot before you touch it.

CHRIS: Are– are the oven mitts hot?

'CHRISTMAS GUY'

PETER: I'm a secret-agent astronaut millionaire.
FORMER CLASSMATE: Cool. Where'd you get the cowboy hat?
PETER: Space.
'Patriot Games'

THE MANY FACES OF
PETER

Say what you like about Peter, he's got one hell of an active imagination, and he sure knows how to use it. Wild escapades and misadventure ahead? He's there!

Meet Peter's latest alter ego in Season 13 episode, 'Quagmire's Mom'.

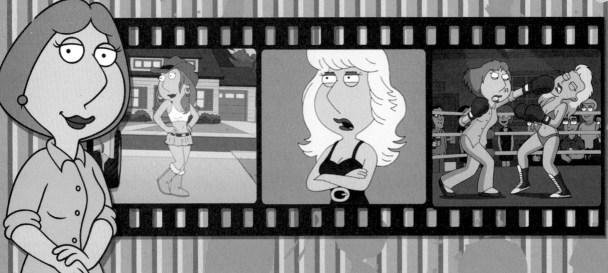

THE MANY FACES OF
LOIS

Lois puts up with a lot, and Peter's crisis-causing antics test her limits, but she's a true fighter, and real classy with it. He'd better watch out!

LOIS: I'm going through a phase... where I'm only attracted to handsome men.
'North by North Quahog'

THE MANY FACES OF

BRIAN

BRIAN: Hey, Peter, it's seven o'clock and you've still got your pants on. What's the occasion?
'Death Has a Shadow'

Look out for Brian's brand new look in Season 13 episode, 'Brian the Closer'.

Whoever said Brian was a pretentious pseudo-intellectual almost certainly didn't see him in banana-mode... Hey, ladies, he's a fun guy!

Stewie may be confused about his identity, but that's resulting in some stylish sartorial choices! That big-brained baby's got talent - and he knows it, yeah?

THE MANY FACES OF

STEWIE

STEWIE: I don't wear anything I can't take off with a flourish.
'Brian's a Bad Father'

9

CHRIS

What Chris lacks in brains, he makes up for in enthusiasm. Seems to be working out pretty well – apart from the 'danger to himself' thing… Haha!

RON (MEG): I've gotta go buy razors. you know, for my beard.

THE MANY FACES OF

MEG

One day, Meg may stop being the family scapegoat (is that too much to ask, Peter?) Maybe she'll ditch that hat for good. Not for a while, though!

THE MANY FACES OF

JOE

Joe takes his cop duties seriously, even when it's his friends causing the trouble.

MEG GRIFFIN
IT'S A FAMILY THANG

THE MANY FACES OF
QUAGMIRE

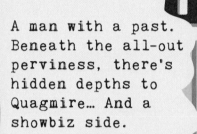

A man with a past. Beneath the all-out perviness, there's hidden depths to Quagmire… And a showbiz side.

He's very big in France, apparently!

"I like where this is goin'! Giggidy, giggidy, gig-gi-dy!"

Look out for Joe's authorly alter ego in Season 13 episode, 'The Book of Joe'.

THE MANY FACES OF
CLEVELAND

You can count on cool-guy Cleveland for words of wisdom - even if it takes him quite a while to get those words out… And he's got moves!

JOE: I'll take smelling good over walking good any day.

BONNIE: You don't smell good, Joe.
'Meg Stinks'

Peter's Pictures

How to Take the Perfect Selfie

Peter's no stranger to the selfie, as you can see for yourself right here - and also online: **@peterpumpkineater69.**

Discover Peter's amusing captions for these images there, but before you do that, why not think of your very own hilarious hashtags and descriptions - then find out how they compare?

TIP 1: It's all in the lighting!

TIP 2: Find your best angle!

#...

#...

STEWIE: Oooh, you took a black and white picture of a lawn chair and its shadow and developed it at Save-On. You must be so brooding and deep.

'Whistle While Your Wife Works'

TIP 3: Show off your assets!

BUS

#...

TIP 4: Keep it colourful!

#..

TIP 5: Choose an 'arty' background!

#..

TIP 6: Don't forget that selfie stick!

#..

TIP 7: Be creative!

#..

TIP 8: Reveal your fun side!

#..

TIP 9: Persistence pays off with the perfect shot!

#..

#yolo #awkward #fomo #nofilter #tbt #yo

New Year's

If you're reading this around Christmas time, hope you're making the most of the holiday fun, because once January arrives, it's all change... You're about to become a new person overnight!

It's goodbye gluttonous old ways, financial mismanagement, bad ol' booze, and that snooze-you-lose procrastination - That was '2015 you'. '2016 you' will be someone else entirely!

Who better to prepare you for a brand new year than the Griffins? Let's look back at how not to do it - with a couple of oh-so useful tips and tricks to help you on your way...

Get Fit!

In the brand new episode, 'The Book of Joe', Brian takes up running to impress a woman, and immediately gets hooked on that endorphin high. Pretty soon, he takes it all a bit too far...

He's not the first of the family to feel the buzz of getting active. Or, to take things to an unhealthy extreme. Remember when his buddy Stewie beefed up, with some dangerous bodybuilding, in 'Stew-Roids'?

STEWIE: It doesn't matter how you find the pot of gold, B to the rian.

All that matters is that you beat the leprechauns.

'STEW-ROIDS'

There was also that time Peter headed to local gym, 'The Sweaty Clam', after a fight with an octopus made him realise how out of shape he was.

And when Peter took Chris to get fit, in 'He's Too Sexy for His Fat', he ended up getting some 'work' done, on himself, instead. First, to get thin - and then to develop some no-effort muscles...

Tip! Don't cheat – there's no substitute for hard work - and don't overstretch yourself. It's never a good idea to climb Mount Everest on no training...

Look out for Quagmire's unusual 'workout' in new episode, 'Our Idiot Brian'!

Quit Smoking

What's the deal with smoke breaks? If you smoke, you get to legitimately have half the day off... That's the conclusion Peter comes to at work, in 'Secondhand Spoke'. He manages to convince his boss, Angela, that he's a smoker - and quickly becomes addicted, with a ruinous effect on his health and appearance. Doctor Hartman can't help him – as if! – and when Peter finally decides to stop, and wants to return to normal, he can't.

Even cutting to a shot of the outside of the house, with music – which normally works – doesn't help him.

Tip! Somehow, Peter has since returned to how he was, so surely quitting can only be a good thing.

Resolutions

Give Up the Booze

In 'Peter's Two Dads', his alcohol consumption led to an unfortunate unicycle accident, as 'Pee Pants the hobo clown', causing the ultimate demise of Francis Griffin, the man Peter believed to be his father.

With "you're a fat, stinking' drunk" probably still ringing in his ears, Peter has since gone on to cause further inebriated chaos, and things got serious in 'Friends of Peter G' - when Death arrived in Quahog to show Peter what his life would look like both on and off the booze...

Tip! Don't go getting hooked on energy drinks instead. Remember what happened to Peter in 'New Kidney in Town'...?

Live a Life of Zen

Being 'mindful' is, like, so now. Or you could scrap that and do what Peter does...

> PETER: We all got anger, Chris. The important thing is finding a healthy way to channel it. For me, as you know, it's the family bath.
>
> *'12 and a Half Angry Men'*

Sort Out the Finances

By which we don't mean "remortgage the house and spend the lot on lottery tickets", like Peter did - twice – in 'Lottery Fever'.

Live Life to the Full

It's time to make every day count. Stewie's realising this, after some not-so-subtle digs from Brian in 'This Little Piggy'. And Joe? Well, let's just say he's about to seriously change his lifestyle, in another Season 13 episode - the brilliantly titled '#JOLO'.

Oh, my stars!

HOROSCOPES

FOR 2016 ★★★★★★

PETER: HEY, LOIS, HOW MUCH DO YOU THINK A SAGITTATIUS PAYS? LOIS: I THINK YOU'RE IN THE WRONG SECTION PETER.

'PETER'S PROBLEMS'

YOU'RE ON THE CUSP OF GREATNESS, PROBABLY. ALL OF YOU. BUT BEFORE YOU MAKE ANY BIG DECISIONS THIS YEAR, WHY NOT CHECK WHETHER YOUR CHARTS ARE ALIGNED. EXPECT THAT OBLIGATORY REFERENCE TO URANUS...

IT'S GONNA BE AN EXPLOSIVE YEAR!

ARIES MAR 21 - APR 19

When the working day is done, Aries just wants to have fun. Sadly, that garbage won't take itself out. Oh, and there's groceries to get, obviously, and if you want a job doing properly.... You're fiery, impulsive and independent, which is a polite way of saying you like to argue. A lot. If you relax a bit in March, big things are set to happen, involving a fire truck and an idiot loved one.

TAURUS APR 20 - MAY 20

Taurus! You're strong, tough, patient and dependable. You'd make an excellent cop. Funny, that. This year, time to finally sort out that relationship that's been troubling you. Failing that, ignore it a bit more, and spend time hanging out with your buddies. Make sure they're irresponsible types, for added drama. Road trip, you say? ROAD TRIP!!

GEMINI MAY 21 - JUN 21

You're the sign of the twins – and it appears, in your case, that one of them is evil.

Gemini, it's time, this year, to work out who you really want to be. Go all out, with costumes, hairpieces and funny props. You have to see it to be it. And if you wear that hat you'll be seen for miles! In other advice, indulge your whims this winter.

Just watch that pronunciation.

QUAGMIRE: WHAT CAN I SAY? I'M A VAGITTARIUS. OH! ★★★★★

'MEET THE QUAGMIRES'

CANCER JUN 22 - JUL 22

Cancer! Buddy! You have quite a year ahead, that's for sure. But it's all looking pretty unpredictable. Maybe one morning you'll decide to buy a camel, or a pimped up new car. Next Wednesday, though, it's certain: roller-skating, followed by a pony trek.

LEO JUL 23 - AUG 22

Lookee here, Leo. You may be the big lion at work, but ditch the ego at home, and learn to play the pussycat for once. In other – ahem 'news', watch out for that crafty co-worker who you just know has their eye on your job. Rarrrrrr! Oh, and you know you had that big dream once? Maybe spend some time on that. November is your month to shine.

VIRGO AUG 23 - SEP 22

Hey, Fussy McFussington, it's not all about appearances, you know. Take that critical eye, and use it to look inward. As in, at yourself (what did you think I meant? Weirdo). I predict new breakthroughs for you in July, when your softer side comes to the fore and your relationships improve no end.

Get you!

LIBRA SEP 23 - OCT 23

Light-hearted Libra, there's more to you than meets the eye…

You may not care what other people think, but underneath the silliness is… well, let's just say that, this year, you should keep that firmly under wraps, and go about your official business.

SCORPIO OCT 24 - NOV 21

Whattup, water baby? So needy… You're too old for these extreme emotions, and – seriously - it's becoming hard work. You're relentless, obsessive, jealous. You feel things deeply. Forever. February brings you great news on the romance front. Cruelly dashed by the middle of the month.

SAGITTARIUS NOV 22 - DEC 21

Check you out, Sag. This year, your popularity knows no limits. Which is why you'll find yourself handcuffed to a department store bed at opening time… probably some time around June. Why not take off somewhere fancy this year and meet new people. Everyone in town already knows you intimately.

CAPRICORN DEC 22 - JAN 19

Hey there, Capricorn, you old goat. You're pretty witty, when you're not whining. Stop working so hard and live a little, this year. While you're about it, those health niggles you've been worrying about? Get them looked at pronto, before something drops off.

AQUARIUS JAN 20 - FEB 18

Off the wall, or what? You are 'unique', and that's probably a good thing. You're ruled by Uranus. But we knew that. Don't think too much this year, and everything will be AWESOME! Awesome. Explore your creativity in May, and who knows what may happen…

PISCES FEB 19 - MAR 20

Compassionate and oh-so romantic… This year is the year for lovin'. Use that famed Piscean intuition, why dontcha? You're a psychic sponge. And speaking of sponges, this is also the year for bathroom remodeling.

17

A YEAR IN QUAHOG

CHRISTMAS

CHRIS: I love the Christmas Carnival! LOIS: Chris, calm down. You're giving yourself a nosebleed.

'Christmas Guy'

Other holidays are available, but for the Griffins, it's all about this one. Not least because of the emotional events of 'Christmas Guy' - and, of course, Peter's story in 'Jesus, Mary and Joseph!'

However you spend your festivities, try not to flip out, like Lois, in 'A Very Special Family Guy Freakin' Christmas'. And if you're thinking of saving Santa, keep an eye on Stewie (the flashbacks to that present drop off in 'Road to the North Pole' keep on coming...).

It's Christmas in Quahog in the new episode, 'The 2000-Year-Old Virgin'. Peter's old pal, Jesus, is back! And he knows exactly what he wants for his birthday...

NEW YEAR

New Year parties never go to plan. So, sometimes, the best resolution is to stay at home. Remember the Griffins' Y2K scare? They saw in the Millennium with a bang - from their basement - in 'Da Boom'. That was sixteen years ago... They made it. Happy 2016!

VALENTINE'S DAY

Love is in the air... and when the residents of Quahog get romantic, they really go for it. As witnessed, rather voyeuristically, in 'Valentine's Day in Quahog'. That was when all of Brian's exes turned up at once, Quagmire discovered his feminine side, Stewie was drawn to that mysterious girl, and Meg had her best date ever...Which was also technically her worst.

Top tip: try not to lose your kidney on a first date.

ST PATRICK'S DAY

If you have Irish roots like Peter, why not head out of Quahog and take a trip back to the old country for an authentic celebration? Be warned, though, Mickey McFinnigan - that's Peter's pop - surely has a headache-inducing night planned. Pace yourself.

EASTER

JILLIAN: I just want some coloured Easter eggs!

'Road to the North Pole'

Chicks and bunnies and eggs. Oh, my! Just make sure you're not getting this egg-cited at Christmas - like Jillian, here. Easter? Eager, more like!

PETER: Valentine's Day... A day of love, right in the middle of Black History Month. There are a thousand hearts in Quahog, a thousand stories. Some people don't have any stories. Others got two. *'Valentine's Day in Quahog'*

CHRISTMAS

NEW YEAR

ST PATRICK'S DAY

EASTER

SUMMER

PETER: I'm half-shark and half-Peter, don't come near me, I will eat you.

'Play it Again, Brian'

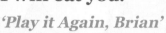

Sometimes, you just have to escape the daily grind. And if you live in Quahog, where better to head for your summer vacation than Martha's Vineyard? That's the thinking for Lois, when our dog of the moment wins a writing prize, and brings her and Peter along to share the glory. Take it easy, but perhaps not as easy as the ever-intoxicated Peter...

FALL

BRIAN: The summer tourists are gone and we finally have the town to ourselves - before the idiots from New York show up to watch the leaves change and take over the whole place.

'Lethal Weapons'

Those words had just left Brian's mouth, then that first leaf changed colour, and Quahog was suddenly overrun with fall-foliage-photo-takers. Aka the "leafers". Ahhh, the change of seasons...

The message is clear: skip town, embrace it, or take a 'leaf' (sorry) out of Lois's book... She knows how to deal with it, in 'Lethal Weapons'.

HALLOWEEN

STEWIE: Y'see these holes? I got bit by a vampire. I'm a vampire duck!

'Halloween on Spooner Street'

If you're heading out trick or treating for the first time, and you're going to be all naïve about it, like Stewie, make sure you have someone suitably scary, like Lois, to watch your back. Those big-kid bullies will think again before they go after another little ducky's candy...

THANKSGIVING

PETER: Aw! This looks fantastic! I can't wait to poop this out!

'Thanksgiving'

Friends, family, neighbours... and, in the case of Brian, awkward ex-lovers. They're who gathered around the Griffin table for a turkey-and-pumpkin-pie feast in 'Thanksgiving'. Then, Joe and Bonnie's presumed-dead son, Kevin, also rocked up. Brian probably gave thanks that the resulting drama took the focus firmly off him and Ida. If you're in a similarly uncomfortable social situation, you could also make use of this kind of 'surprise guest' scenario.

'Turkey Guys' - If Lois is expecting another holiday meal at 2.30 sharp, she'd better think again... This Season 13 episode sees Peter and Brian on a big bird mission. Plus, lots of painful small talk during the long wait for food back at the house.

SUMMER   **FALL**   **HALLOWEEN**   **THANKSGIVING**

THE GIFTS THAT KEEP ON GIVING:
MAKE YOUR OWN MUG

BREAKFAST WITH BRIAN, A LATTE WITH LOIS, A STEAMING CUP OF JOE...?

ALL OF THESE – AND MORE – CAN BE YOURS IN A FEW SIMPLE STEPS. JUST DRAW THEIR MUGS (AS IN 'FACES'!) ON YOUR ACTUAL MUG, AS FOLLOWS...

YOU WILL NEED:

- A cheap, plain white mug – washed thoroughly with soap and water, then dried

- **OIL-BASED** sharpies

- An oven

VERY IMPORTANT!

TO CREATE:

- Simple! Using your sharpie(s), draw your favourite character, or write your favourite quote from the show on your mug.

- Let the design dry for a few hours or, ideally, overnight.

- Put the mug in a COLD oven, then turn it on to 425°F / 230°C / gas mark 8.

- Bake for 30 minutes.

- Turn off the oven and leave the mug in there until it cools down completely, so it doesn't crack (and you don't burn your hands!).

TIPS:

- ONCE FINISHED, THE MUGS ARE HAND WASH ONLY.
- KEEP THE DESIGN AWAY FROM THE EDGE, WHERE YOUR MOUTH WILL TOUCH.
- IF YOU'RE NOT ARTISTICALLY GIFTED, LIKE CHRIS, PRACTICE FIRST ON PAPER.
- EXPERIMENT WITH DIFFERENT COLOURS. BLACK WORKS BEST, OR GO OH-SO FANCY WITH METALLICS!

CAREFUL!
Get help from a responsible human to avoid a Brian-style oven disaster.

THE GIFTS THAT KEEP ON GIVING:
WORLD'S GREATEST FARTER

PETER: MEG, I WANT YOU TO HAVE THIS SAD-SOUNDING FART.

For gassy guys and gals...

Everyone has a special talent - it's just a matter of finding it, then letting it rip!

If you know someone, just like Peter, who's remarkable at rectal turbulence, exceptional at ass exhalation, whose breakthrough skill involves breaking out the brown cloud... well, you get the picture. They've harnessed their own wind power, they've rebuilt the ozone layer one foul howl at a time... and you're bursting to acknowledge their efforts in the field of butt-based fumigation.

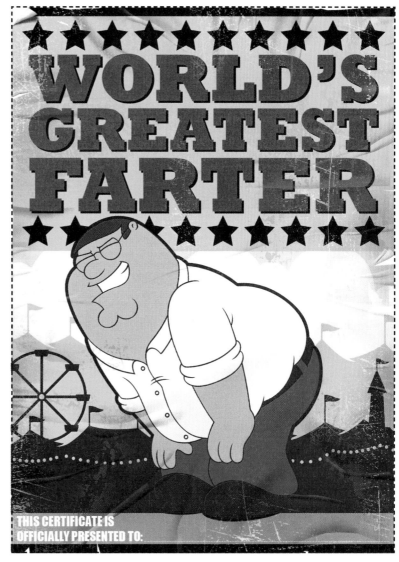

★ ★ ★ ★ ★ ★ ★ ★ ★ ★ ★
WORLD'S GREATEST FARTER
★ ★ ★ ★ ★ ★ ★ ★ ★ ★

THIS CERTIFICATE IS OFFICIALLY PRESENTED TO:

What do you want to give them? A medal? No. Anal applause? Probably (although that's surely more their forté).

This silent-but-oh-so-deadly certificate? Why, certainly!

Cut it out and ensure it has pride of place in their office (or toilet) cubicle!

CAREFUL!
Scissors and jerks! So make sure you get help from a mature adult when using them.

Family Guy and THE BRITS

'Chap of the Manor'

As revealed by Stewie and Brian, in 'Viewer Mail #2', Family Guy is based on British series, 'Chap of the Manor', set in the town of Billingsbury (you've surely heard of it? What do you mean, no?). The plot centres on the family life of Neville and Lydia Griffin and their children, Collingsworth and British Meg. Plus, of course, their pet horse and American baby.

Neville spends all his time with his mates down the pub – no, not "The Fox and Pig and Dog and Wolf and Cat and Fiddle and Whistle and Cock", but "The Dog and Cat and Bull and Whistle and Fiddle and Cock and Pig and Wolf and Carriage and Fife and Other Wolf".

When it's announced that the Queen is coming to Billingsbury, Peter thinks "that's bloody sweet!". He reveals that he's related to royalty - and sets out to prove it…

Also featured in this episode: theatrically introduced cutaways about the rain, a very well mannered pheasant fight, cricket, British coppers and some choice swear words. There's also glimpses of that quintessentially British gameshow, 'Wheel of Politeness'. "Sorry everyone!"

'Chap Stewie'

Of course, if anyone has an affinity with jolly old England, it's certainly Stewie. He's got the voice, for starters - and that voice is based on a famous British actor. Look it up! Which links us nicely to the whole Eliza Pinchley - cockney-turned-'posho' – plot in 'One if by Clam, Two if by Sea'….

When he's not taking tea with Rupert, or having one of his sexy parties (inspired by a certain British comedian, big in the 1960s and 70s), he's catching up with his favourite British TV shows (and there's more on those later).

In 'Chap Stewie', he's reborn into an emotionally repressed, well-to-do, British family - of the kind he's seen on television. Which should be perfect for him, but suddenly he's "the moron" of the family, and he doesn't like it at all.

And in 'Road to Europe' his trip to London doesn't quite play out as expected. Oh, Mother Maggie!

What ho, chaps! Family Guy has a special affection for Blighty, bad teeth and all (no offence...).

Rain, tea, warm beer, and classic comedy cultural references, it's all in there. Let's serve up a selection of the 'best of British' bits, right here...

LOIS: The British are a lovely people. Not physically, of course, but inside...
'One If By Clam, Two If By Sea'

PETER: I say we fight the British and drive them back to whatever country they come from!
'One If By Clam, Two If By Sea'

PETER: Alright, now, listen up, you limey bum sniffers...
'Patriot Games'

Scotland

Like Seth Macfarlane himself, Peter is part Scottish. Did you know that it was Peter's great-great-great uncle, Angus Griffin, who invented golf? There's a fact you need to share!

And who could forget that 'traditional' Scottish chipmunk...?

PETER: Is that right, Scottish Chipmunk? He doesn't talk, but he's a chipmunk and he's Scottish and he would back me up on this.

'The Hand That Rocks the Wheelchair'

Football

Ah, football, the beautiful game... But it's not soccer, it's American football, in 'Patriot Games'. Peter is sent to London to play with the maypole-dancing, pillow-fighting London team, the Sillinannies, at Silly Nanny Stadium. They're as good at the sport as they sound.

Meanwhile, in the Big Smoke, Lois and family experience life in a London flat, plus West End theatre (which only Chris 'gets'). And Stewie takes public transport, but not in the normal way.

Royalty

In 'Peter's Progress', we heard the story of Peter's past life as Griffin Peterson in "England, 1670, or 1760. Whatever". The tale was told of his love for Lady Redbush, and his subsequent rivalry with the (allegedly) equally enamored King Stewart III - who sent Griffin Peterson to the New World, where he founded the city of Quahog...

And, while we're on a theme, who could forget the central role Peter played in a certain famous royal wedding (after he prayed really hard)...? You can witness that iconic occasion, Peter-style, at the end of 'Livin' on a Prayer'.

There are far too many British references in the show to mention them all here – like the London Gentlemen's Club cutaway, in 'Jerome is the New Black' - but keep a lookout and listen closely for some very familiar voices...

British TV shows...

Stewie loves his British TV. We witnessed it first with his Jolly Farm Revue obsession, which has taken him to the show's original London home (in 'Road to Europe'), and onto the American set - as a cast-member in disguise - in 'Go, Stewie, Go!'

British-drama-wise, Stewie was hooked on The Cadwalliders of Essex, a groundbreaking British show about "a wealthy family dealing with slight change" - as shown in 'Chap Stewie'. And, also in this episode, Stewie revealed a sound knowledge of other Brit dramas, namely:

- *The Caduggans of Aubrey Muse*
- *The Whittakers of Edgerton Crescent*
- *The Roysters of Pumbridge-on-Thames*

And in 'Viewer Mail #2', Lois caught a glimpse of obscure arthouse drama, Condensation.

In the season 13 episode 'Stewie, Chris and Brian's Excellent Adventure', their travels lead them to England, 1912, and onto the Titanic...

They also make a stop off to release "pent-up time travel farts" at the home of a famous British author.

MAYOR WEST'S
WEIRD WORDSEARCH

It's all about to take a turn for the surreal, now. Find the red words, uttered by the Mayor himself.

They could be vertical or horizontal, forwards or backwards, or diagonal...

Quickly! Time is running out!

TRISHA
TAKANAWA:
Do you have any words for our viewers?

MAYOR WEST:
Yes... box, toaster, aluminum, maple syrup... no I take that one back. I'm gonna hold onto that one.

'Stewie Griffin: The Untold Story'

"Today we are here to honour Joe Swanson for pulling my poor one-eyed cat **Bootsy** out of the old stove pipe of my Grandmother's cabin."
'Ready, Willing and Disabled'

"My God! My wife is seeing another **mayor**!"
'Valentine's Day in Quahog'

"Well, I'll be damned, and they called me crazy. 'You can't plant **sausage seeds**,' they said. Well look at this!"
'Bill and Peter's Bogus Journey'

"If I enter **Connecticut**, I'm entering every state that Connecticut's ever been with. Good luck, brave travellers."
'Road to Rupert'

"So it's a **shouting match** you want, eh? Well, game on, Quahog! Arrrgh! Arrrrgh! Arrrrgh!"
'The Perfect Castaway'

"My God, I'm a **tomato**!"
'You May Now Kiss the... Uh... Guy Who Receives'

"Oh, God, I love this song! And I love it when amateurs sing the lyrics. But I hate **baseball cards.**"
'Don't Make Me Over'

"Wrong! I'm 95 percent **helium**."
'Road to the Multiverse'

"Oh my God, what a couple of squares! **Squaresville**, I tell ya!"
'And Then There Were Fewer'

CAROL: Hellooo!
MAYOR WEST: Well, dot dot dot **hello**!
'Brothers & Sisters'

MEG: Excuse me, Mayor West?
MAYOR WEST: How do you know my **language**?
'The Story on Page One'

"I love this job more than I love **taffy**. And I'm a man who enjoys his taffy."
'E. Peterbus Unum'

"It's alright, I'll put a **message** in a bottle. Now...we wait."
'And Then There Were Fewer'

MAYOR WEST: Damn I lost him. Alright cats, back in the bag.
Starts putting the cats back in the bag
MAYOR WEST: Come on **Fluffy**, come on **Mittens**, come on **Paul Laughing**. What a ridiculous name for a cat, Paul! That's a person's name – a person's name! Paul!
'Prick Up Your Ears'

```
A L B W S U J A J S L X P Q Z G
C L J M B K C W B E A K L M O V
N U C S H O U T I N G M A T C H
W A D X E F W O W D C P W N D I
S P J F P Z U E S T J Z Q W E Y
S Z G R T Y Q E G A U G N A L U
Q I A R W F I O O P A H S D F G
U H J K M J K L Z X S I C B V B
A L C Z A W X J T V B P N M Y N
R K U J Y H K G F D D S A P F O
E T R E O W Q E E R T Y U V F I
S Y F T R L R E W Q M N B V A C
V X O Z L G K J H O T A M O T M
I Q R N T Y U Y I U H Y R E P Q
L M Q N B V M I T T E N S C I Z
L X Z J L R K J G H F D S A P O
E I S U Y B T R E K W Q E R T Y
P L K J H L G F D S P I C T Y U
D U W H E L I U M M I Y U Y M T
K L E N W X C V B N S M Q E V R
A S D G F H Q W E T R T O Y U O
G P A S D P F G O H J K L Z X C
Q V B N H M Q O E R T Y L U O Y
L Z X C V B B N M L R K E L I P
K J G F D S A P J O I U H Y T R
L K B H F D S A S Q S C W K D Q
V E F T B R L G N T H C M Y J M
W M K I C O N N E C T I C U T U
N F F S G H K O A K U A O X E O
T L M E S S A G E Y E X F N P V
A C G E G I K M O Q S U Y A C E
G I K M N Q E R B T Y X Y G H P
U S X Y C I H V A A B G S L O D
A D U C H F L E S E W Z Q P J U
H E A X W K G W E Q M E O L A R
R E G A B D G O B P U X J W L R
K S L C Z O D F A X A A L C C Y
L E D H E M T F L H A I D S J P
E G L A R J G N L U A T H O N D
A A V F I A O S C P F H I L F I
F S A G C E A I A H P F L E P D
R U I Q D C H A R E N G Y E H L
T A Y I R C U L D L V Y D N L A
B S D F H J L B S M N Q J E S R
```

CUTAWAYS

cutaways cut·a·ways   *noun, plural*

1. Flights of fancy, random recollections, surreal non-sequiturs…
In Family Guy, anything goes!

Everyone has their favourite cutaway gags from the show. Here are just a few of the finest.
Who could forget…

When Peter tried that energy drink for the very first time, and it sent him on a Queen-of-Pop high…

"And I feel…!!!"
'New Kidney in Town'

When Joe became a different person (and thought he was in a different show)…

"Good morning, USA!"
'Foreign Affairs'

When Peter extolled the virtues of the State of Massachusetts, in song…

"Oh, I'm intoxicated alright, Lois."
'Play It Again, Brian'

When Lois and Bonnie went sightseeing in Paris…

"Can we at least do some Muppet-style sightseeing first?"
'Foreign Affairs'

When Peter was late for school, eighties-movie-style…

"That's the power of love!"
'Baby Not on Board'

When we found out how the Evil Monkey became evil…

"Honey, good news! I made partner!"
'Ready, Willing and Disabled'

When Peter had a part-time job at a fast food joint (and a special song)…

"DING! Fries are done!"
'Deep Throats'

When Peter got revenge on that pigeon that pooped on his car…

"That's right… Get it nice and clean…"
'Back to the Woods'

When Peter got excited when they said the title of the movie IN the movie…

"He said it! He said it!"
'Episode 420'

And when Stewie set up a cutaway, but there was no clip…

"They'll come after you like Peter went after that hockey coach. Oh? No clip? Nope? Thought we had a clip."

'Saving Private Brian'

When Peter kept Lois up all night, "writing with that giant plume of his"…

"Dearest Augustine, I do hope this latest damp has not aggravated your grey lung.

Dib-dib-dib."

'Mr & Mrs Stewie'

How about that time Peter worked as a team?

"Man, I hope he lets me on his team this year. I haven't been part of a team since I was with the Four Peters."

'Model Misbehaviour'

Or, those two weeks he spent narrating his own life…

"I looked with a grimace at the questionable meal Lois had placed in front of me. Of course, I'd never tell her how disgusted I was with her cooking, but somehow I think she knew."

'Peter Griffin: Husband, Father… Brother?'

Some of the funniest cutaways in Family Guy are about, well, cutaways!

Those 'meta' moments include…

When Stewie and Brian travelled back to the very first episode, and witnessed the 'behind-the-scenes' spooky Griffin pauses, where the cutaways went…

… And compared that to what they do during the cutaways now…

BRIAN: Oh my God, is that what we did back then?
STEWIE: Yeah, I mean, now we just, like, return text messages and screw around and whatnot.

'Back To the Pilot'

… Then travelled five years into the future, to find the show had advanced animation, but the writing had got lazy…

PETER: Chris, I heard you got a "D" on your report card.

(Peter looks at the camera)

Here's a cutaway.

'Back To the Pilot'

DOCTOR, DOCTOR...

They say laughter is the best medicine, which is just as well, because what Dr. Elmer Hartman lacks in professional training and competence he sure makes up for in (unwitting) comedy!

Here's a selection of his mirth-making medical mishaps.

DR: Alright, I'm just going to put on a pair of gloves and we'll deliver this baby. [Sticks hand in box] These don't feel like gloves at all… They feel like used needles.
'Emission Impossible'

LOIS: Will you just tell us how Peter's health is?
DR:… Now, onto the cancer. You are a cancer, right? You were born in July? Now, on to these test results. My, they're much worse than I thought. My son got a D minus on his history test. Now, Mr Griffin, that liver's got to come out. It's been in the microwave for three minutes, it'll get dry.
LOIS: Please, please, we can't take anymore schtick. Please, just tell us, is Peter healthy?
DR: Oh yeah, he's fine. He's just really fat.
'The Fat Guy Strangler'

DR: Mrs Griffin, I'm afraid he'll never walk again… without remembering how lucky he is that he'll only be in this wheelchair for two weeks! That leg should heal up just fine.
'No Meals on Wheels'

DR: Mr and Mrs Griffin, I'm afraid your coma's in a daughter. I mean your daughter's in a coma! What?! Oh my God! Did you- did you hear what I said! Brain freeze! Oh my God, that one is going in the Christmas letter!
'Peter's Daughter'

[Lois has a broken nose.]
DR: Is it cool if I tell your insurance that I gave you heart surgery?
'Baby, You Knock Me Out'

DR: It's a girl! With a penis and no vagina.
'Yug Ylimaf'

DR: Y'see that Diploma? Yale Medical School.
MEG: Wow, that's impressive.
DR: Thank you, I work very hard on my calligraphy.
'You Can't Do That on Television, Peter'

PETER: Oh my God, what happened?
DR: You were in a coma, and then I kissed you and you woke up. But two days later.
'Viewer Mail #2'

LOIS: Please, doctor, you've got to help him. You took an oath when you went to medical school.
DR: I took a lot of things when I went to medical school.
'Ratings Guy'

LOIS: Dr Hartman, is Peter going to be okay?
DR: Ugh! If one more person asks me about a patient today, I'm gonna scream.
'Total Recall'

Perhaps the biggest mishap of them all…

Dr: I once tried to clone a chicken. The result wound up being a man-sized chicken that was incredibly hostile and ended up escaping from the lab.
'New Kidney in Town'

A FAMILY GUY BINGE WATCH FEAST

Back-to-back episodes lined up? You seriously need some snacks!

For something more substantial, you no doubt already have 'Hurry Up, Shrimp' on speed-dial – or there's always 'McBurgertown', of course...

Quahog Stuffies

Hey, clam fans...In celebration of the city of Quahog, and the edible hard-shell clam it was named after, here's a tasty treat to make founding father, Miles 'Chatterbox' Musket, oh so proud!

Before we start, some clam tips:

To store: Refrigerate in a bowl covered with a damp cloth as soon as possible after buying and use within 24 hours.

Before cooking: Wash the clams well. Scrub under cold running water with a stiff brush, discarding any that have broken, cracked or open shells - or any that do not close when tapped firmly.

Can't get hold of fresh, large clams? You can also make this with canned minced clams (use one can, drained of all but 1 tablespoon of clam juice). Bake, as directed below, on clam shells - or in a casserole dish, to be enjoyed as a dip, with bread, crackers, or whatever you fancy!

Ingredients:
- 10 large Quahog (or chowder) clams
- 3 tablespoons minced onion
- ½ cup / 110g butter
- 2 tablespoons chopped fresh parsley
- 1 clove garlic, crushed
- 1 tablespoon lemon juice
- 1 cup / 60g fresh bread crumbs
- 1 tablespoon clam juice (or cooking liquid from steaming the clams)
- Salt and pepper to season
- ¼ cup / 20g grated parmesan

Instructions:
- Preheat oven to 350ºF/ 180ºC / gas mark 4.
- Fill a large pan with 2 inches of water, and bring to the boil. Add the clams to the boiling water and reduce the heat to a simmer. Steam the clams for 7-10 minutes, until the shells open.
- Remove clams from the pot and cool them enough to handle. WARNING! Throw away any clams that have not opened - these should NOT be eaten.
- Remove the clam meat from the clams and mince them.
- Break apart the clam shells from their hinges. Rinse and pick 10-12 of the best-looking shells. Set them aside.
- In a saucepan, melt the butter on medium heat and add the minced onion. Once softened, add the garlic. Cook for a minute, then add the parsley, bread crumbs, clams, lemon juice, and clam juice. Stir until the stuffing mixture is completely moistened. (If it's dry, add more butter or clam juice; if too wet, add more bread crumbs.)
- Place the clam shells on a baking tray, and a little stuffing mixture onto each one. Add grated parmesan on top, and bake for 20-25 minutes, until the cheese is lightly browned.

PETER'S WIFE'S CKIES

And in honour of Lois and Peter's brand new business in 'Baking Bad', here's a very special recipe - sure to be a favourite with the freakin' sweet-tooth in your life...

Ingredients:
- 1 cup / 225g butter
- 8 oz / 225g cream cheese
- 2 eggs
- 2 teaspoon vanilla essence
- 1 ¼ cup / 220g brown sugar
- 2 cups / 280g self-raising flour
- 1 cup / 80g cocoa powder
- ¾ teaspoon baking soda
- Pinch of salt
- 1 cup / 80g chocolate chips
- 1 cup / 150g roughly crushed chocolate brownies/brownie pieces (store-bought, or home-baked)

Instructions:
- Preheat oven to 350ºF/ 180ºC / gas mark 4.
- In a bowl, cream together softened butter, cream cheese and sugar. Add eggs one at a time, plus the vanilla.
- In another bowl, combine flour, cocoa powder, baking soda and salt. Carefully mix dry ingredients into butter mixture. Beat until combined.
- Stir in chocolate chips and brownie pieces.
- Chill dough for an hour.
- Line baking sheets with parchment paper. Roll dough into balls. Lightly flatten to form your cookies.
- Bake for 10 minutes. Remove and let cookies rest on baking sheets for 2 minutes. Remove to a cooling rack.

"OH, AWESOME! MMM. MMM. OH, MY GOD, TH-THESE ARE DELICIOUS."
Peter Griffin

If like Peter, you should in no way be near boiling water, sharp knives or ovens, get a responsible adult to help. Or sit back, watch TV and let them do it all instead!

WHAT THE HELL?!

Here's a look back at some classic "What the Hell?!" moments.

You may have spotted that this exclamation appears in almost every episode...

Can you guess which episodes these 'W.T.H' moments are from?

1 ....

2 ....

3 ....

4 ....

5 ....

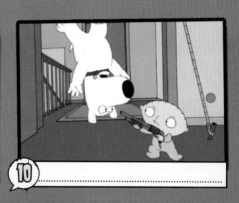

6 ....

7 ....

8 ....

9 ....

10 ....

EPISODE TITLES

Vestigial Peter   **To Live and Die In Dixie**   **Boys Do Cry**   **Quagmire's Baby**

Prick Up Your Ears   **Not All Dogs Go to Heaven**   **Barely Legal**

Brian: Portrait of a Dog   **Call Girl**   **The Courtship of Stewie's Father**

BRIAN'S BRAIN

STEWIE: "Check out the big brain on Brian!"

'The Big Bang Theory'

Pomposity, thy name is Brian...

In celebration of 'Our Idiot Brian', who takes a trip to the dumb side in Season 13, it's time to look back at some of the douchiest and most pretentious examples of what Stewie calls Brian's "superficial quasi-knowledge..."

We love Brian, but sometimes, well... Wow.

On Stewie's play...
STEWIE: Hey, Brian.
BRIAN: Uh, hey, Stewie.
STEWIE: Listen, have you seen my play?
BRIAN: Y'know, Stewie, I have seen your play, and it is exhilarating to me. A child's play is one of the most beautiful things in the world. Continue to play, little one. You're our future.
STEWIE: What the **** are you talkin' about? The play I wrote. Have you seen it?
'Brian's Play'

On Brian's play...
"The American play was dying. Have we brought it back to life here? I can't say that, but it has a pulse."
'Brian's Play'

On a day's work...
BRIAN [AT LAPTOP, WRITING]: A writer who inherits a magic typewriter that writes for him, but then it turns out the typewriter is... racist? Totally makes sense. Older technology, older worldview. [Closes laptop] And that is a good day. I earned some banana bread.
'Brian's a Bad Father'

On working...
PETER: Y'know, Brian, you could get a job.
BRIAN: I have a job. I-I'm a writer, Peter, I'm working right now. S-see this? All of this? This is the raw material of a picture of life that I'm gonna paint with words.
PETER: Yesterday it took you thirty minutes to lap up a cold cut off the floor.
BRIAN: That's my process!
'Peter's Problems'

More on that...
FAN: What's your process?
BRIAN: How do I even answer that? Uh, what's a rainbow's process? Two parts rain, one part sun, one part childlike wonder. What we do know though, is that the end result in both cases is joy.
'Brian's Play'

On his impending unemployment...
"You can't fire a writer in the middle of a show. That'd be like a doctor leaving in the middle of a surgery!"
'Brian's a Bad Father'

In the Writers' Room...
HEAD WRITER: Alright, guys, before we begin today, I want to introduce our newest staff writer, Brian Griffin.
BRIAN: Hi guys! Yes, I am that Brian Griffin. You probably have my novel, but just so you know, in here, I'm just one of the guys. Alright?
'Brian's a Bad Father'

BRIAN [REJECTING AN IDEA]: No, no, no, guys, guys. Come on. Where's the stwistusion? (silence) Really? Really? I'm the only guy here who's heard of that? Stakes, twists, conclusion. Stwistusion.
HEAD WRITER: That sounds made up.
BRIAN: Let me ask you something. Are you afraid right now?
HEAD WRITER: What? No!
BRIAN: That's what's wrong! You should be, y'know. Art is scary! This is writing, man!
'Brian's a Bad Father'

Brian's dialogue for kids' show, 'Parent Boppers'...
GIRL: My stupid parents want me to wear a bike helmet!
BOY: Parents are lame!
DYLAN [AS DJ]: Hold on, other kids. Maybe they just recognise that nothing can protect us from the tedium of our mundane lives. Aren't we all on bikes without helmets?
DIRECTOR: Cut! Your line is 'that's right, Cameron.'
'Brian's a Bad Father'

This one time...
"This one time I attended a speakers' colloquium on federal judgeships..."
'Whistle While Your Wife Works'

Emotional expression...
"I texted him S-R-Y, frowny face. I mean, he knows that I'm sorry. And that I'm sad."
'Brian's a Bad Father'

STEWIE'S ABCS

In the new episode, 'This Little Piggy', Stewie 'graduates' from the green room to the purple room at preschool. To celebrate this proud occasion, we're looking back at a whole alphabet's worth of memories of our brainy baby.

A 'An American Marriage'

The play Stewie writes, inspired by his pal's success in 'Brian's Play'. "My God, it's miraculous!" - is Brian's verdict of the work, behind Stewie's back. But to his face? "It wasn't good."

B Bertram

Stewie's arch-nemesis and half-brother, via blundering Peter's sperm-bank disaster, in 'Sibling Rivalry'. Victory shall be Bertram's, apparently. But we've yet to see it.

C Cool Whip

Or "Cool Hwhip", as Stewie is determined to pronounce it, much to Brian's annoyance. This gag was spawned when Meg made her seriously sinister pie, in 'Barely Legal'. There have been several callbacks to it since.

D Da Vinci, Leonardo

Artist, inventor, the ultimate Renaissance man... Da Vinci is also Stewie's ancestor - as revealed in 'The Big Bang Theory'. "Of course! My love for spaghetti-os and smoking on the toilet! It all makes sense!"

E England

With that accent and affinity for Blighty-based TV, you'd think England would still be Stewie's spiritual home. But his experiences in 'Road to Europe' and 'Chap Stewie' may have put him off.

F Fictitious Housekeeper

If you ever need to RSVP to a party planned by Stewie, you may get to speak to the high-pitched Mrs Pennyapple - who sounds, surprisingly, kinda like her baby-faced employer. Brian discovered this in 'Peter's Two Dad's'.

G Gorgeous Randy Flamethrower

Let us never forget Stewie's "dodgeball pseudonym", as revealed in 'Brian's Play'.

I "I don't like change!"

Stewie's understandable, but very funny, reaction to Peter ripping out a whole chunk of the Griffin house to construct the Quahog's Men's Club, in 'Believe It or Not, Joe's Walking on Air'.

H Hilarious Laugh

"That's not baking powder, it's sneezing powder!" said the TV. And cue Stewie's infectious response. Or, as Brian puts it:

"That messed up way that you laugh when you think something's really, really funny".

'Brian Sings & Swings'

J

STEWIE JUST SAID THAT!

Jingle

STEWIE: Y'know, Brian, you may be a dog, but you're a pretty cool cat.
SINGERS: Stewie just said that!
STEWIE: Take it home with ya!
'Seashorse Seashell Party'

K

Knock, Knock...

STEWIE: Knock, knock
BRIAN: Who's there?
STEWIE: Your friend, Stewie. And he's always gonna be there for you.
'Stewie B. Goode'

L

Lois

The mother-son relationship may be a love-hate one (at least on Stewie's side), but they've come a very long way since Family Guy began. He's eased off on the matricidal urges.

M

Mother Maggie

Never meet your heroes, so they say. But Stewie didn't listen. A trip to England, and the TV show, Jolly Farm Revue, in 'Road To Europe' brought shocking revelations.

N

Novel

When Brian's not working on that novel, Stewie's reminding him.

"How you uh, how you comin' on that novel you're working on? Huh? Gotta a big, uh, big stack of papers there?"
'Brian the Bachelor'

O

Owl

When Stewie wants to give Brian unsolicited love-life advice on the down low, there's only one outfit for the job. Twit twoo!

"Don't do it, Brian! Take it slooooow!"
'Love Blactually'

P

Penelope, Olivia, Julie, Janet...

Baby Stewie's had his fair share of playground - and child star - crushes. And who could forget that doomed marriage to his old rival, Olivia...

Q

Quite confused

... but Stewie has plenty of time to figure out who he really is.

In the meantime, we'll embrace his experiments! Look out for his revealing speech in 'Turkey Guys'.

R

Rupert & Oscar

Stewie and Rupert have been through a lot together. But when his old bear, Oscar, reappeared, Stewie began to question everything...

S

Stu Griffin

There's a glimpse into Stewie's possible future in 'Stu & Stewie's Excellent Adventure'. It's not quite what he'd had in mind...

T

Time Travel & Tea Parties

When Stewie's not travelling through time, there's always a tea party to be had. It's thirsty work, quantum physics...

U

UV Rays

"Tan Stewie" soon learned the dangers of "getting his bronze on", in 'The Tan Aquatic'. But at least he got to ballroom dance with Brian. "Olive juice you, too."

V

Vascular

When Stewie hit the gym, with some worrying help, he became buff and, well, incredibly 'vein'...

"Look how vascular I am, Brian. If there's one thing women love, it's a vascular man."
'Stew-Roids'

W

Weapons Room

Stewie and wicked baby Penelope bonded over their respective weapons rooms, in 'Mr & Mrs Stewie'. He thought he'd met his soul mate, until it all went horribly wrong...

X

Is for Kiss

A trip back to the 1960s saw Stewie fall for the cutest baby. They shared a moment, until Carter came to collect his little Lois.

Y

Yellow Cake Uranium...

Z

Zzzzzz...

SPOT THE DIFFERENCE

Think you're an 'eagle'-eyed, difference-spotting pro? Well, let's see shall we?

It's time to – ahem - 'putt' that to the test, right now!

LOIS: … since you like golf, I thought we could play a round. S-so…what do I do, just aim for the pond?

'Dr C. & the Women'

YOUR ANSWERS HERE!

1. _____
2. _____
3. _____
4. _____
5. _____
6. _____
7. _____
8. _____
9. _____
10. _____

MISSING MEG

IT'S TRUE: IN HER HOME AND SCHOOL-LIFE, MEG RARELY 'FITS IN'. BUT SHE'S DOING A PRETTY GOOD JOB OF BLENDING IN HERE. CAN YOU FIND HER?

"I'M JUST TRYING TO FIT IN!"

DOUBLE TAKE
DOUBLE TAKE

Lookalikes, evil twins and very freaky clones. Plus your favourite characters dressed up as one another. No need to get your vision checked. Just enjoy!

STEWIE: My name's Peter, and I work in the brewery. Now I'm gonna put on my pants and talk to my co-worker's a... these pants have stool in them.
'Ratings Guy'

O'BRIAN: Whose leg d'you have to hump to get a pint of Guinness around here?
'Peter's Two Dads'

STEWIE: I've been so damn busy lately, my schedule's been so packed, I felt like I needed some kind of an errand boy to do all my nit-picky pain-in-the-arse stuff. So I cloned myself.
'Quagmire's Baby'

Over the seasons, Peter's been blessed with twins. Who could ever forget his plucky double, Chip (in 'Vestigial Peter')? Or how about his two, quite different, dastardly doppelgängers, Thaddeus Griffin (in 'Mother Tucker') and Retep (in 'Meg Stinks!')...? Oh, and there's also that hairless twin who lives in the storm shed (in 'Fresh Heir')...

37

Your Family Guy
NAME GENERATOR

Your name is so freakin' boring! If you're after an exciting alias, are searching for a pseudonym, or need a nom de plume, like, now, check out these ludicrously brilliant character suggestions. Either take the hint and pick the first and last names next to your own initials, or break these rules entirely (you little rebel), and mix and match your own...

	FIRST NAME	LAST NAME	
A	Colonel	Goatbanger	'Cool Hand Peter'
B	President	Douchebag	'Stu & Stewie's Excellent Adventure'
C	Livingston	Winstofford	'Brian Goes Back to College'
D	Fjurg	Van Der Ploeg	'Tales of a Third Grade Nothing'
E	Stink	Fleaman	'Airport '07'
F	Wavyhaired	Douchein	'Quagmire and Meg'
G	James	Bottomtooth IV	'No Chris Left Behind'
H	Detective	Scrotes	'Stewie Griffin: The Untold Story'
I	Smiley	McGee	'Stew-Roids'
J	Hannah	Banana	'Hannah Banana'
K	Sergeant	Extreme	'Saving Private Brian'
L	Major	Awesome	'Saving Private Brian'
M	Sneakers	O'Toole	'Boys Do Cry'
N	Fielding	Wellingtonsworth	'Brian Goes Back to College'
O	Eliza	Pinchley	'One if by Clam, Two if by Sea'
P	Wellesley	Shepherdson	'Brian Goes Back to College'
Q	Amelia Bedford	Furthington Chesterhill	'Brian Goes Back to College'
R	Kent	Lastname	'Friends Without Benefits'
S	Dick	Pump	'Halloween on Spooner Street'
T	Shelley	Boothbishop	'There's Something About Paulie'
U	Lee	Keybum	'The Simpsons Guy'
V	Lady	Cadwallider	'Chap Stewie'
W	Buzz	Killington	'Whistle While Your Wife Works'
X	Viscount James	Earl Tennisracquet	'No Country Club for Old Men'
Y	Duke of	LaCrosseteam	'No Country Club for Old Men'
Z	Reginald B.	Stifworth	'There's Something About Paulie'

What's your new name? ....

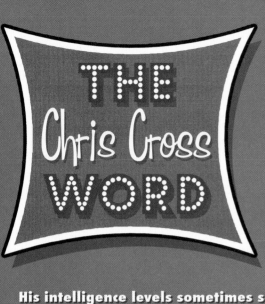

THE Chris Cross WORD

"Cool, I don't have to go to school. I can just pee in my bed all day!"

'No Chris Left Behind'

His intelligence levels sometimes seriously let him down, and even put everyone's lives at risk - like in the brand new episode, 'Stewie, Chris & Brian's Excellent Adventure'... But Christopher Cross Griffin is about to test your smarts with this, his very own puzzle. Yaaay!!

ACROSS

9. Who helps Chris to beat the bullies in 'Secondhand Spoke'? **(6)**

11. What's the name of the dead cat Brian gets Chris for Christmas in 'Bill and Peter's Bogus Journey'? **(6, 4)**

12. Who voices the teacher Chris falls in love with in 'Fast Times at Buddy Cianci Junior High'? **(4, 9)**

16. In which month is Chris's birthday, according to the episode, 'German Guy'? **(8)**

17. Who voices his Lois-lookalike girlfriend in 'Tom Tucker: The Man and His Dream'? **(5, 4)**

20. What's the name of Chris's goth band in 'Saving Private Brian'? **(6, 3)**

DOWN

1. What's the name of the fancy school he's sent to in 'No Chris Left Behind'? **(7, 4)**

2. What's the full name of Chris's smitten neighbour? **(4, 7)**

3. What job does Chris originally do in Quahog? **(8)**

4. In which episode does Chris become the sole heir to the Pewterschmidt fortune? **(5, 4)**

5. What does Peter sell to help pay for Chris's school fees in 'No Chris Left Behind'? **(4, 10)**

6. What 's the first thing Chris really wants for Christmas in 'Road to the North Pole'? **(1, 4, 2, 6)**

7. Which actor voices Chris? **(4, 5)**

8. What's the name of the teacher Chris falls in love with in 'Fast Times at Buddy Cianci Junior High'? **(3, 8)**

10. What's the name of the animated TV pilot Chris creates with Peter, in 'FOX-y Lady'? **(5, 6)**

13. Which creature was a long-time fan of Chris's closet? **(4, 6)**

14. Which creative skill is Chris particularly talented at? **(7)**

15. What present does Chris receive at the end of 'Road to the North Pole'? **(6)**

18. What's the name of his Lois-lookalike girlfriend in 'Tom Tucker: The Man and His Dream'? **(7)**

19. What is the name of Chris's girlfriend – Jerome's daughter - in 'Baby Got Black'? **(3)**

Quagmire's QUICK QUIZ!

Think you know Glenn? Well, it's time to find out. Giggity, Giggity, Goo!

QUAGMIRE

PRIDE OF QUAHOG

1. AN EASY ONE TO START...
   WHAT'S QUAGMIRE'S OCCUPATION?

....

2. IN WHICH COUNTRY IS HE FAMOUS AS AN
   ACTOR, AS SHOWN IN 'BIGFAT'?

....

3. AND WHAT'S THE NAME OF THE FILM HE
   STARS IN?

....

4. WHAT'S HIS REAL SURNAME, AS
   REVEALED IN 'TIEGS FOR TWO'?

....

5. WHO IS THE LOVE OF HIS LIFE?

....

6. WHAT'S HIS DAD'S ORIGINAL NAME?

....

7. WHO DID HIS DAD BECOME?

....

8. WHAT'S HIS MOM'S NAME?

....

9. AND HIS SISTER'S?

....

10. WHICH IT PRO DID HE GET INVOLVED
    WITH IN 'QUAGMIRE'S QUAGMIRE'?

....

11. WHAT'S THE NAME OF HIS FEMININE
    ALTER EGO IN 'VALENTINE'S DAY
    IN QUAHOG'?

....

12. WHAT NUMBER SPOONER STREET DOES
    HE LIVE AT?

....

13. WHAT'S THE NAME OF THE MUSICAL
    ACT HE FORMS WITH PETER IN
    'IN HARMONY'S WAY'?

....

14. WHO IS HE MARRIED TO IN
    'MEET THE QUAGMIRES'?

....

15. WHO DOES HE MARRY IN
    'THE GIGGITY WIFE'?

....

16. WHO DOES HE MARRY IN 'I TAKE
    THEE QUAGMIRE'?

....

17. WHAT KIND OF ANIMAL DOES QUAGMIRE
    PREFER AS A PET?

....

18. WHAT IS HIS DAUGHTER'S NAME,
    FROM 'QUAGMIRE'S BABY'?

....

19. WHAT'S THE YEAR OF HIS BIRTH,
    AS REVEALED IN 'FOX-Y LADY'?

....

20. HOW DOES HE STAY LOOKING SO YOUNG?

....

21. WHERE DOES HE BUY HIS FAMOUS RED
    HAWAIIAN SHIRTS, AS REVEALED IN
    'QUAGMIRE'S QUAGMIRE'?

....

22. WHAT'S THE NAME OF HIS ALTER
    EGO, AS REVEALED ON A PHONE
    CALL TO LOIS IN 'AIRPORT '07'?

....

Finished? "Alriiiight!" You can Quagglechek the answers (a clue, there), on page 61!

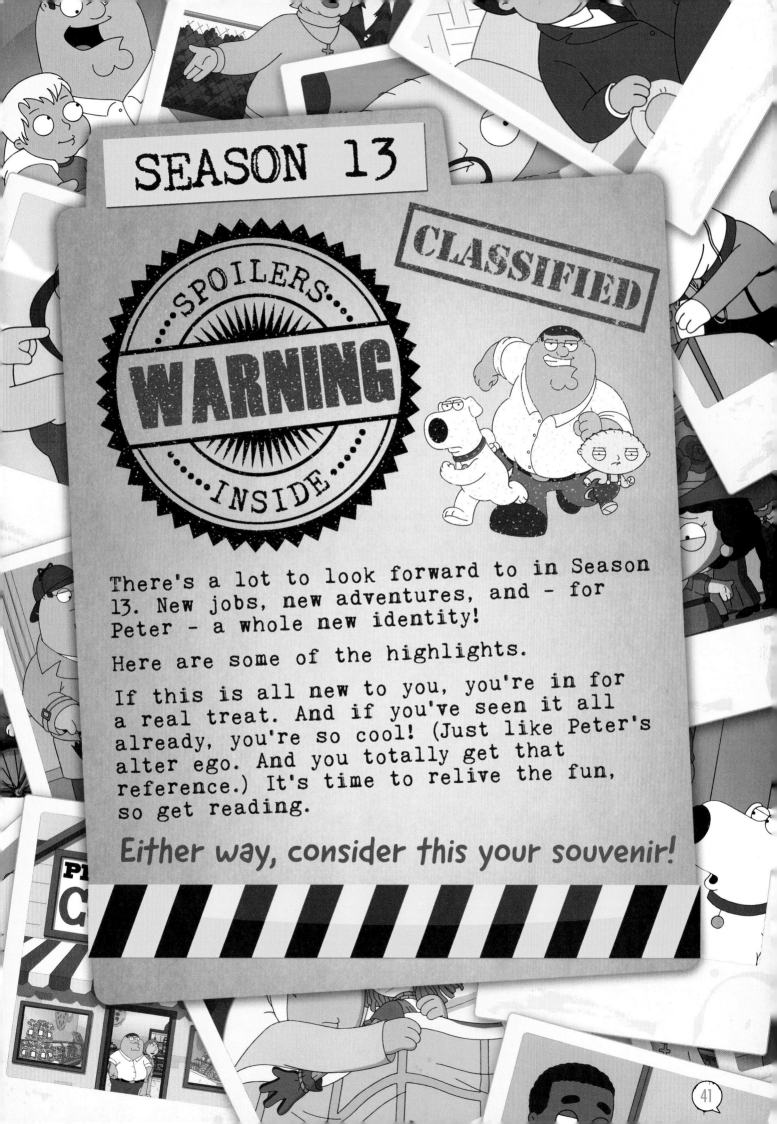

SEASON 13

SPOILERS WARNING INSIDE

CLASSIFIED

There's a lot to look forward to in Season 13. New jobs, new adventures, and - for Peter - a whole new identity!

Here are some of the highlights.

If this is all new to you, you're in for a real treat. And if you've seen it all already, you're so cool! (Just like Peter's alter ego. And you totally get that reference.) It's time to relive the fun, so get reading.

Either way, consider this your souvenir!

Writing's a Marathon, Not a Sprint...

Joe is a man of hidden talents, as Peter learns when he stumbles across illustrations for his pal's unpublished children's book, 'The Hopeful Squirrel'. Joe's been working on it for nine years, and Peter convinces him that the world should finally see it. But their friendship is put to the test when Peter becomes the 'face' of Joe's work.

Meanwhile, in the pursuit of romantic interest from a runner called Chloe, Brian attempts to pass himself off as a fellow athlete. But he gets a little too hooked on that euphoric 'runner's high', and takes things a bit too far...

Things to look out for:

- Joe's awesome pen name
- That ghostwriter cutaway
- Brian's band-aids — count 'em!
- Peter's preferred reading matter

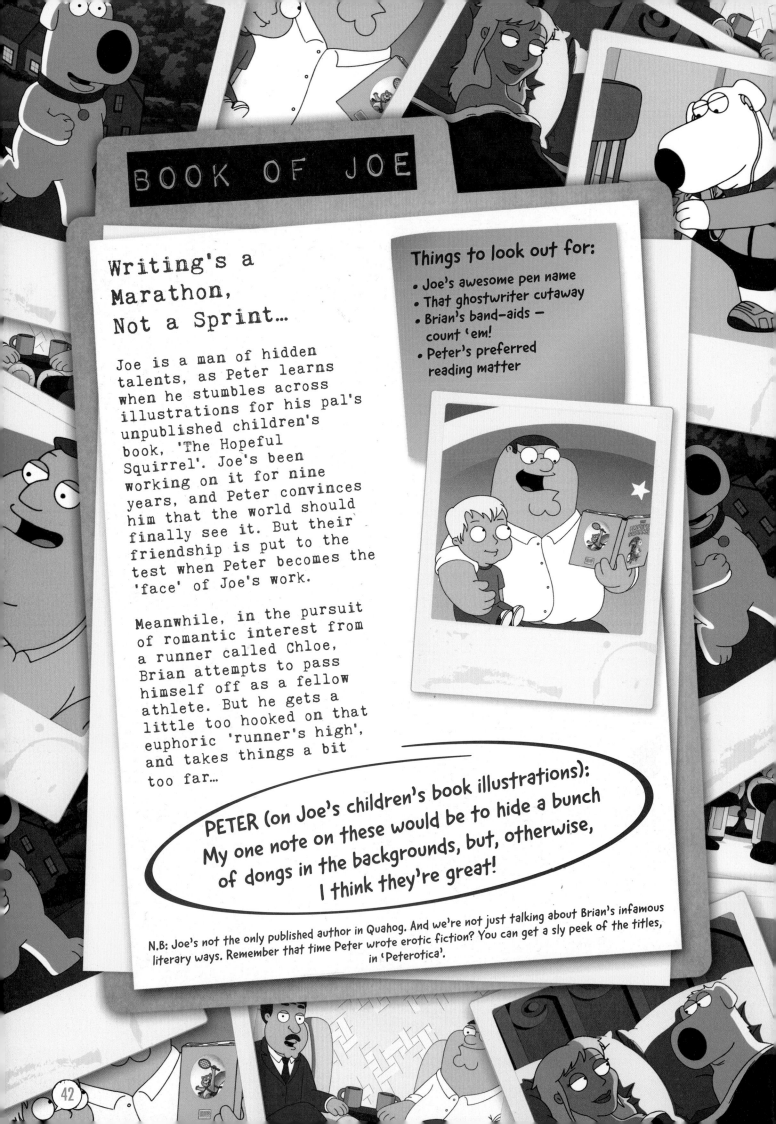

PETER (on Joe's children's book illustrations): My one note on these would be to hide a bunch of dongs in the backgrounds, but, otherwise, I think they're great!

N.B: Joe's not the only published author in Quahog. And we're not just talking about Brian's infamous literary ways. Remember that time Peter wrote erotic fiction? You can get a sly peek of the titles, in 'Peterotica'.

Peter's Wife's Cookies

When Lois organises a charity blood drive, Peter learns of his wife's exceptional baking talents - her cookies are incredible! Inspired, he convinces Lois they should open their own store.

Business hat on, Peter's all for 'thinking outside the box', but when Quagmire convinces him that 'sex sells' - and Peter runs with the idea - Lois is not happy.

Meanwhile, insomniac Stewie gets a little help in the falling-asleep department, from his good friend, Brian. But it turns out that adult cough medicine is addictive...

LOIS: You know, we did so-so building a family, but this business — I think we can really knock it out of the park.

N.B: This is not the first Griffin food business. Who could forget 'Big Pete's House of Munch', in 'No Meals on Wheels'?

Things to look out for:

- The so-familiar bank supervisor
- Stewie's under-the-influence bathtime
- Peter's success speech
- Quagmire's 'unearned giggity'

Lying through his teeth...

After Brian's face is badly injured in an accident caused by Peter - who really, really wanted Brian's chewy rope toy - Quagmire cannot bear to hear his old nemesis's toothless talking, so pays for Brian's new dental work.

With a winning new Hollywood smile, Brian accidentally lands a job in real estate.

The ensuing success goes to his head, and Brian is persuaded to take on his most difficult property challenge yet, convincing his new pal and benefactor - yep, that's Quagmire - to buy a real dump...

N.B: We know how Quagmire feels about 'pretentious', 'textbook liberal' Brian. It all came out in that rant in 'Jerome Is the New Black'...

Things to look out for:

- 'Precious' Peter
- Brian's movie star teeth and sales montages
- Quagmire's 'workout'
- Peter's pointy hat song

LOIS: Brian, we can try to make you feel a little less repulsive (*chuckles*) but we're not spending human money on a deformed animal.

Turkey Day Trouble...

When Peter and Brian drunkenly eat the Thanksgiving turkey the night before the big day, and show Lois the photographic evidence to prove it, she is not impressed. It's okay though, because Peter can easily get a replacement festive bird, right? Wrong!

Cue an epic mission to track down that elusive turkey - and get home in time for the main event.

Meanwhile, with Peter gone AWOL, Stewie convinces his big brother, Chris, that he must step up and become the 'man of the house'. But Chris struggles to cope with the responsibility...

N.B: If it's an uninterrupted, on-time Thanksgiving feast you're after, don't go to the Griffins'. It was all going so well last time, until Kevin Swanson rocked up (in 'Thanksgiving')...

Things to look out for:
- Peter's pictures posted online: **@peterpumpkineater69**
- Brian's not pretentious-at-all voicemail message
- Stewie's revealing Thanksgiving speech

PETER: There's our answer. We break into the zoo, steal a turkey, bring it home, we're heroes.

The Story of the Virgin Birthday...

It's Christmas Time in Quahog, and Peter runs into his old pal, Jesus, in the mall. Jesus invites Peter over to his place, but when Peter sees the Messiah's squalid apartment, and remembers Jesus' birthday is coming up, he feels sorry for him and decides to throw him the best party ever.

But, when planning the party, Peter and the guys find out that Jesus has never ever had sex. So, instead, they make it their mission to find him the right woman, with whom to 'get biblical'...

N.B: Peter and the Son of God go waaaay back. You may remember their friendship was formed after "mass awareness of a certain avian variety", in 'I Dream of Jesus'...

JESUS: Hey, Peter. Come on in. Mi casa es, uh... I–I don't know Spanish.
PETER: Huh, I think half the world would be surprised to know that.

Things to look out for:

- The speed-dating montage
- Stewie's Christmas wrapping
- What the 'H' in 'Jesus H. Christ' stands for
- Peter's erotic advent calendar

Going Down in History?

Chris is not doing well at school, and if he doesn't pass his history final, he'll have to repeat 9th grade. So, when Stewie sees quite how badly Chris is struggling, he decides to give him a real-life history lesson - with Brian in tow - courtesy of his time machine.

During their adventure through the past, Stewie comes to the conclusion that Chris is actually a moron - and tells him so. Chris storms off, ending up on the ill-fated maiden voyage of the Titanic...

N.B: Stewie's increasingly taking Chris under his wing. Like that time he stepped in to stop his big brother getting bullied, in 'Secondhand Spoke'...

Things to look out for:

- Stewie's 'sex joke'
- The Lois–Peter texts
- 'The entire 1990s'
- Rupert's disclaimer

CHRIS (to Stewie): That's why victory is always Brian's.
STEWIE (to Brian): You dick! How much of my stuff have you taken credit for?!

Who's a Clever Boy?

Meg's seriously freaking out about her SATS, so when her friends suggest she gets someone else to take her test for her, Meg butters up Brian with flattery. After praising his novel, 'Faster than the Speed of Love' (which she has SO not read), he's in! Successfully disguising himself with the trademark Meg hat-and-glasses combo, he takes the test.

But the results are back - 'Meg' comes bottom of her class. Brian is devastated, but Peter convinces him that being stupid is great. They spend a fun-filled and mindless day together - Peter-style - and, pretty soon, Brian begins to fit in…

Things to look out for:

- Peter's 'good luck message' for Meg
- The 'Roaring Twenties' song
- Peter and Brian's 'idiot' montage
- The dog in space cutaway

N.B: Meg's not the only family cheater. Remember that time Brian himself got 'help' on an assignment (from another Griffin), in 'Brian Goes Back to College'?

PETER: Hey, look, don't feel bad, Brian - it's fun being stupid. You don't got to worry about nothing, you don't got to read books, and you never die.

Meg Gets a Foot in the Door...

When Meg is offered work as a model, she's surprised and overjoyed... Until she discovers the kind of photographs intended - foot fetish porn. But when she quickly becomes an internet sensation, Meg decides to embrace it anyway. Popular, at last! She may be keeping the nature of her work under wraps, but secrets have a habit of getting out...

Meanwhile, Stewie takes heed of Brian's complaint that today's kids get a certificate for everything, but don't actually achieve anything, and decides to take a year off, to "live life to the fullest". But there's trouble ahead, when, at a music festival, Stewie and Brian both fall for the same woman...

PHOTOGRAPHER: Listen, you probably get asked this all the time, but have you ever modelled?
MEG: I've never even been in a picture before.

NB: It seems Meg does take after her mom, after all. Remember that time Lois pursued her own modeling ambitions, in 'Model Misbehaviour'?

Things to look out for:
- Peter's big excuse to get out of everything
- What Peter and Lois get up to in private
- Meg's birth
- Stewie's attempts to get comfortable

Like Mother, Like Son...

When Peter learns that his 'chequebook' is really just a blank pad of sticky notes from Lois, he demands the real thing.

But, at the bank, a bigger surprise is in store, when he discovers that 'Peter' is actually his middle name - and his first name is really Justin. This changes everything! Peter decides he's going to live a cool, younger, 'Justin lifestyle'.

After a house party at 'Justin's', Quagmire's illegal sexual exploits catch up with him, prompting the giggity one to face up to his past...

Things to look out for:

- Peter's karaoke cutaway
- Justin's 'sweet news wall'
- Peter's birthday surprise
- Quagmire's ABCs

BANK MANAGER: Hi. What can I do for you?
PETER: Yes, I was wondering, where is the room where I can roll around nude with my money?
BANK MANAGER: I'm sorry?
PETER: No, I'm sorry. I thought this was a bank.

N.B: Peter's not the only Griffin to go through this kind of phase — tattoos and all.
Remember Mrs G's mid-life crisis, in 'Lois Comes Out of Her Shell'?

THINK INK!

CREATE YOUR OWN TEMPORARY TATTOOS

IF YOU'D LIKE TO LIVE PETER'S 'JUSTIN LIFESTYLE'. BUT DON'T WANT A PERMANENT REMINDER OF THAT TEMPORARY FEELING. HELP IS AT HAND. HERE'S A TEMPORARY REMINDER. INSTEAD! TAKE YOUR PICK FROM THIS 'KEWL' SELECTION OF GRIFFIN GRAPHICS...

YOU WILL NEED

✳ TRACING OR PARCHMENT PAPER
✳ A PENCIL
✳ GEL PENS IN YOUR DESIRED COLOURS
✳ A CLOTH
✳ WARM WATER

INSTRUCTIONS

✳ TRACE THE DESIGN ONTO THE PAPER USING THE PENCIL.

✳ FOR DESIGNS WITH WORDS: FLIP THE PAPER OVER AND TRACE THE WORDS WITH A GEL PEN. THE WORDS WILL BE BACKWARDS. BUT WHEN YOU PUT IT ON. THEY WILL BE FACING THE RIGHT WAY.

✳ THOROUGHLY COLOUR IN THE DESIGN USING GEL PENS. GO OVER EACH SECTION SEVERAL TIMES.

✳ PLACE THE PAPER. INK SIDE ONTO SKIN. IN THE EXACT SPOT YOU WANT YOUR TATTOO.

✳ PRESS A DAMP CLOTH FIRMLY ONTO THE DESIGN AND HOLD FOR AT LEAST TWO MINUTES - MAKE SURE NO WATER GETS UNDERNEATH THE PAPER.

✳ GENTLY AND CAREFULLY LIFT UP A CORNER OF THE PAPER. TO SEE IF THE DESIGN HAS 'TAKEN' ONTO YOUR SKIN.

✳ IF IT HASN'T. HOLD THE CLOTH OVER IT FOR A BIT LONGER.

✳ ONCE DONE. REMOVE THE CLOTH AND SLOWLY PEEL BACK THE PAPER.

✳ LET THE DESIGN COMPLETELY AIR DRY.

✳ BE THE TEMPORARILY COOLER. HIPPER NEW YOU!

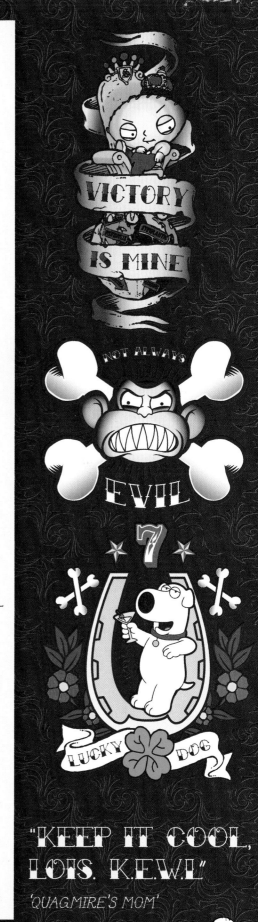

"KEEP IT COOL, LOIS. K.E.W.L."

'QUAGMIRE'S MOM'

Peter Griffin: Private Dick

When Stewie's tricycle is stolen, Peter pretty swiftly takes on - and cracks - the case. It seems he's finally found his true vocation in life, so he decides to open a children's detective agency with the guys.

But then, the trail of a Quahog crime spree leads Peter close to home, and what he discovers soon starts to have serious ramifications on his marriage. If only Peter could use his skills in detection to pick up on the not-so-subtle clues from Lois and actually get the hint...

N.B: It's not the first time Peter's had a mystery to solve. Things were a little more sinister in 'And Then There Were Fewer'...

Things to look out for:

- The computer game cutaway
- Chris's 'creative' calendar
- Joe's 'creative' voicemail message
- Peter's 'creative' sax solo...

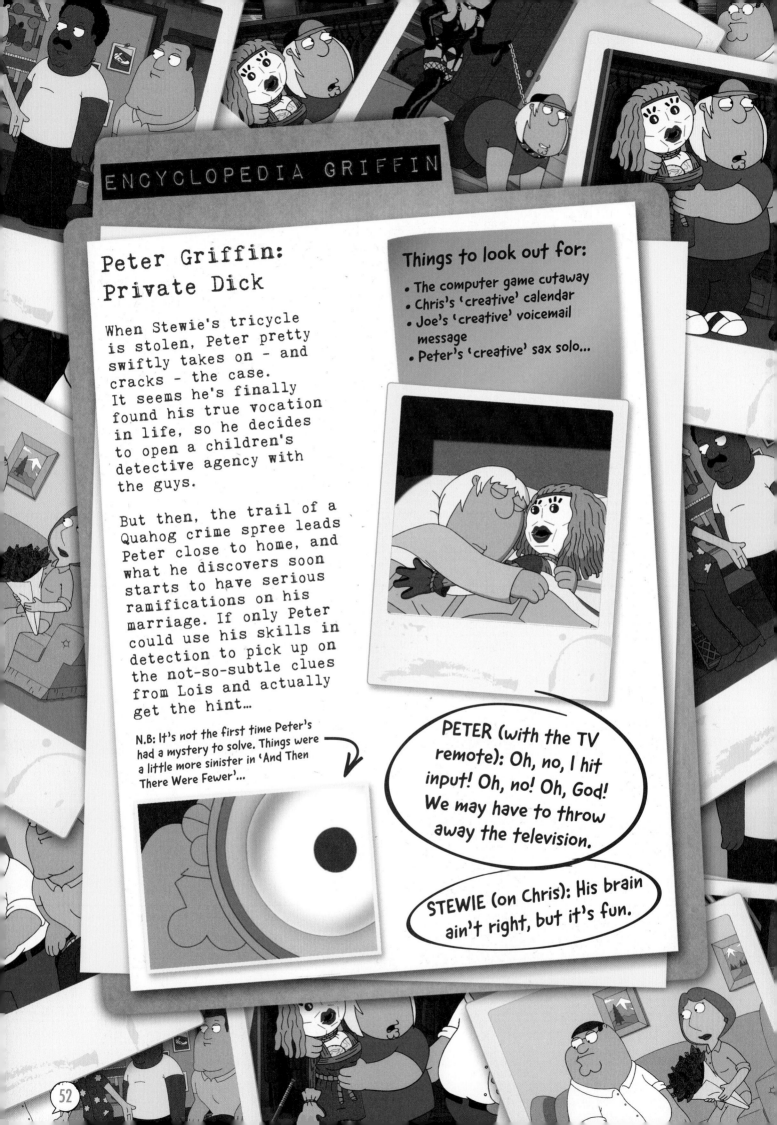

PETER (with the TV remote): Oh, no, I hit input! Oh, no! Oh, God! We may have to throw away the television.

STEWIE (on Chris): His brain ain't right, but it's fun.

He's Having a Baby...

Stewie feels abandoned by an increasingly distant Brian, so when he sees how Susie has brought Joe and Bonnie together as a couple, he hatches an exciting and surely fail-safe plan - He'll have a baby! First, though, the small matter of getting pregnant. And telling Brian. Then giving birth. Oh, and being a parent for the next eighteen-plus years...

Meanwhile, Peter and the guys decide they're going to go viral! It's video brainstorming time, but coming up with a likes-and-shares-inducing internet idea is harder that it looks...

> STEWIE: Is this about money? Because I have a bit saved. We could even use my old crib.
> BRIAN: You use your old crib!
> STEWIE: Oh, right.

N.B: While Peter and Lois are shown as a loving couple before Stewie's birth in 'Chap Stewie', remember when Peter put the pressure on the newborn to save their marriage, in 'Yug Ylimaf'..?

Things to look out for:
- Texting at the table — so rude!
- The viral video brainstorm
- Joe's incredible impressions

Cleveland Finally Finds His Vocation...

When Quagmire and Joe get into a heated fight about which is the best ocean – the Pacific or the Atlantic – Cleveland quickly diffuses the situation. Peter is impressed, so convinces his pal to set up as a therapist. But when Peter persuades an angry Lois to seek Cleveland's professional help, the results aren't to his liking...

Meanwhile, Meg's out to make some cash, so Quagmire gets her a job in airport security. But her newfound status as the hottest woman there doesn't go down too well with another employee...

Things to look out for:

• Cleveland's "horrendous" debt levels
• His Mayor West conclusion
• The squid cutaway
• The end of the show...

PETER: Wow, Cleveland. You calmed them down just by talking with your mouth and your pretty lips.

NB: Meg's not the only Griffin to work at the airport. Remember when Stewie did that brief stint, in 'Stu and Stewie's Excellent Adventure'?

No More Thinking, Just Living...

After Peter unintentionally rescues a missing child, from a pudding billboard, he's hailed a hero and given the key to the city. Joe, who's never been applauded, despite his years of service as a cop, decides his time on the planet so far has been meaningless. So, he chooses to live life the 'Peter way', instead. He quits his job, leaves Bonnie, and becomes a brand new Joe!

Exciting adventures lie ahead. But, when Peter and the guys take a trip to Niagara Falls with their transformed pal, they learn, too late, that Joe has a very different plan in mind...

Things to look out for:
- Peter's band practice
- Joe's fashion history
- Brian's new look

PETER: Awesome, road trip! I love being super pumped for fifteen minutes and then bored out of my mind for eight hours.

NB: This isn't the first time Joe's quit the force and questioned the meaning of his life. Remember that time, in 'Ready, Willing and Disabled', when he "lost the perp", but with Peter's help went on to sporting glory?

Bad Dog!

Brian's drinking has finally caught up with him, and he can't stop puking. When the vet gives him two options, quit the booze, or take some pills, it's a no-brainer – the pills win. But, out of Brian's earshot, Peter learns that he's the man who must administer them. Anally. After several attempts to trick Brian, Peter gets an alarming reaction from his canine pal – resulting in a trip to Obedience School... Meanwhile, Chris makes a new friend in Neil Goldman, but soon learns that Neil has an ulterior motive – named Meg, of course!

NB: Meg and Neil... This sorry saga is ongoing. Who could forget that oh– so beautiful helicopter smooch, as witnessed in 'The Kiss Seen Around the World'..?

Things to look out for:

- 'Pete-in-the-box'
- The family meeting
- The 80s teen-movie cutaway
- Stewie at college

PETER: All right, Brian, it's time for you to take one of these pills from the vet.

BRAIN: Oh, yeah, right. Can we do what we normally do, where you roll it up in a piece of cheese like you're fooling me?

PETER: Yeah, I guess, but then you're gonna have cheese in your ass.

The Joke's on Peter

When Peter witnesses a comedy 'roast' on TV, he's excited and wants to be 'man of the hour'. So, he ropes in all of Quahog to make the gags at his expense. But, at the lavish, Quagmire-hosted event, things get a bit too personal for Peter's liking. He can't take a joke, and, upset and insulted, decides he now needs new pals.

Finding new friends is trickier than Peter anticipated, but, eventually, he stumbles across a brand new and exciting gang who invite him to join them. Soon, though, he's discovering what they're really like…

Things to look out for:
- Peter's sneeze
- Peter's conscience
- The wolf cutaway
- The diving cutaway

NB: When he's not the butt of his buddies' humour, Peter is quite the comedy fan. Remember his search for origins of the greatest dirty joke ever, in 'The Splendid Source'?

BRIAN: You want to have a roast?
PETER: Yeah! Look, he's the man of the hour. Everybody loves him. They got his picture in a circle. How do they do that? Pictures come in squares.

Hollywood Comes To Quahog

Excitement is in the air! Not only is Quagmire hosting 'Quagfest' - a three-day festival, celebrating his one thousand sexual conquests - but also, a huge Hollywood star is shooting a movie nearby. Peter is so unimpressed by the big-screen tough-guy, and his friends are so over Peter's drunken brags that he could "totally kick his ass". So, they challenge him to put his claims to the test…

NB: Peter and fights, eh? It all started with that Giant Chicken, who became Peter's nemesis after giving him an expired coupon, in 'Da Boom'…

Things to look out for:

- Peter at the opera
- Quagmire's 1,000th conquest
- Peter's feminine disguise
- The hush-hush confession

Marital Bliss?

Lois, Bonnie and Donna have a big surprise for their other halves - they've booked a relaxing vacation in the Bahamas. Quagmire wants in too, but it's couples only, so he quickly gets together with Kimmie, who he met "in a pop-up window on the internet". But, once they arrive, it quickly transpires that Peter and the guys have been tricked into attending a couples counselling retreat...

Meanwhile, Carter is in charge of looking after his grandkids (and Brian). Frustrated by their modern-day screen addictions, he sets out to teach them all the joys of "old-timey fun"...

Things to look out for:

- The 'carrier owl' cutaway
- Stewie and Brian's internet ratings
- That oh-so-familiar Bahamian music...
- Peter's beach volleyball

> LOIS: Oh, my God, this place is gorgeous.
> PETER: Yeah, I can't wait to puke up a club sandwich in the pool.

NB: A romantic location, plus relationship troubles? Sounds kinda like the time the gang went on that sunset boat trip, in 'The Cleveland-Loretta Quagmire'...

GOODBYE FROM THE GRIFFINS

Well, that's it for another year. It's certainly been eventful...!

But, don't you worry, there's plenty more Family Guy fun left to be had. Why not take a Peter-style selfie, or two? Toilet pose: optional. Perhaps relive every other cutaway (or WTH?! moment) ever created and compile them in your very own, specially ranked, colour-coded database? That could take a while...

Or, maybe make more Mayor West mugs than you could ever possibly drink from. We think he'd approve.

Whatever you choose to do next, it's pretty safe to say that you're officially set up for an awesome 2016.
You're welcome!
See you
next time...

ANSWERS

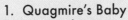

24-25 MAYOR WEST'S WEIRD WORDSEARCH

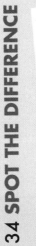

```
A L B W S U J A J S L X P Q Z G
C N U C S H O U T I N G M A T C H
W A D X E F W O W D C P W N D I
S J F P Z U E S T J S D E W E Y
S Z G R T Y Q E G A U G N A L
Q I A R W F I O O P A H S D F G
J L K M J K L Z X S I C H M Y N
E L C Z A W X J T V B P N M Y
K U J Y H K G F D S A S E R O
T R E Q W B T R E W Q M N B V A
R J T R L R E W Q M N B V A C
V X O Z R L G K J H O T A M O T
Q R N T Y U Y I U H Y R E C I
M Q N B V M I T T E N S C I Z
L L X Z J L R K J G H F D S A P O
P L K J H L G F D S P I C T Y U
D U W H E L I U M I X U Y M I
K L E N W X C Z M S M Q E V M
A S D G F H Q W E R T O Y U O
G P A S D P F G H J K L Z X C
Q V B N H M Q C E R T Y L U O Y
L Z X C V B N M L R K E L I P
K J G F D S A P J O I U H Y T R
L K B H F D S A S Q S C W K D
V E F T B R L G N T H C M Y J
W M K I C O N N E C T I C U T U
N F F S G H K O A K U A O X E O
T L M E S S A G E Y E X U F Y A
A C G I K M N Q E R B T Y X Y G H
U S X Y C I H V A A S P S L O D
A D U C H F L E S E W Z Q P J U
H E A X W K G W E Q M E O L A R
R E G L A D G D O B P U X J W L K
K S L C Z O D F A X A A L C C Y
L E D H E M T F H A I D S J P
E G L A R J G N L U A T H O N D
A A V F I A O S C P F H I L F
F S A G C E A I A H P R L E P D
R U I Q D C H A R E N G Y D N L
T A Y I R C U L D L V Y D N S A
B S D F H J L B S M N Q J E S R
```

30 WHAT THE HELL!?

1. Quagmire's Baby
2. Vestigial Peter
3. Barely Legal
4. Boys Do Cry
5. Not All Dogs Go to Heaven
6. Brian: Portrait of a Dog
7. To Live and Die In Dixie
8. The Courtship of Stewie's Father
9. Call Girl
10. Prick Up Your Ears

34 SPOT THE DIFFERENCE

35 MISSING MEG

40 QUAGMIRE'S QUICK QUIZ

1. Airline pilot
2. France
3. 'Monsieur Oops'
4. Quagglechek
5. Cheryl Tiegs
6. Daniel "Dan" Quagmire
7. Ida Davis
8. Crystal
9. Brenda
10. Sonja
11. Glenda Vagmire
12. 29
13. Griffin and Quagmire
14. Lois
15. Charmisse
16. Joan
17. Cats
18. Anna Lee
19. 1948
20. Carrots
21. Ryan's Hawaiians
22. Long Rod Von Hugendong

39 CHRIS CROSS WORD

Crossword answers include: MRS, APAIROFSKATES, FRESH, HEAD, HEIR, STINKYHEAD, LOCKHART, JOHNHERBERT, SETHGREEN, PAPERBOY, BUTTSCRATCHERS, STEWIE, MORNINGWOOD, DREWBARRYMORE, DEVILMONKEY, DIQUACKS, FEBRUARY, DRAWING, RABBIT, ELLENPAGE, PAM, LINDSEY, SPLASHLOG

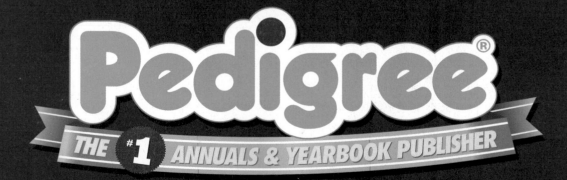